WEDDING PULLS

WEDDING PULLS

poems

J.K. DANIELS

HUB CITY PRESS
SPARTANBURG, SC

First printing, September 2016
Book Design: Meg Reid
Proofreaders: D. Gilson & Rachel Richardson
Printed in Dexter, MI by Thomson-Shore
Cover Photo © Jennifer Shaw

TEXT Baskerville 9.8 / 14
DISPLAY Bebas Neue

Library of Congress
Cataloging-in-Publication Data

Daniels, J. K., 1967-
Wedding pulls : poems / J.K. Daniels.
Spartanburg, SC : Hub City Press, 2016.
LCCN 2016028293 | ISBN 9781938235238
1. Title.
  PS3604.A53337 A6 2016
  811/.6—dc23
LC record available at https://lccn.loc.gov/2016028293

186 West Main St.
Spartanburg, SC 29306
1.864.577.9349

www.hubcity.org
www.twitter.com/hubcitypress

for Karen

CONTENTS

ANCHOR

NOTES

ACKNOWLEDGEMENTS

Thruster holding me tight and that I hold tight!
We hurt each other as the bridegroom and the bride hurt each other.

Walt Whitman, "Song of Myself" (1855)

among fluted columns gilded cupids convex mirrors of the hotel bar
     your fasting to fit the dress red velvet cushions
Rosalind and her new husband enter   hair translucent as chicken broth
wavy antebellum windows   a glass in your hands
scratchy crinolines tight dyed shoes   she kisses you in the bathroom
         lips the raw pink of carved beef
you pull the thimble from the wedding cake
       batten down your buttons old maid
     the bouquet's falling
marbled foyer rug unraveling your leather sole slipping
 drink-fuddled spinning there's no expiation by alcohol *lordhavemercychild*
Lord have mercy in the dooryard lilies *come unto me* the blank pink of scars

THIMBLE

among the finest sepulchers
      City Park carousel
            a saddle of crawfish red   a gilded griffin chariot-laced
      and her foraging for the forearm vein
you find the what-might-have-been-if
    you'd kept your eyes on Glory rather than on Her finest haberdasher
                                  Rosalind's hands
                            rolling brims of felt

outflanked by the radio preacher's incessant threatening   *landslide for God*
      you did not want to be a bride but would have been
            the very thread ribbon crinoline   to be so handled

Rosalind unpitying
    might splint your sprained fingers but won't accept their supplications
                      her terrier's gruff huffing
                        under the table
Dieu not *deux*   you say I *know*   *no*

she keeps the bedclothes fast between you
      unfastens   her headdress to keep the feathers from   your hands
                reine du soliel   your head at her feet
          her papier-mâché bust of Scarlet   *I will never*

Ain't that a shame   Fats Domino in four squares framed in the foyer
                            the slate roof's leering
    you're the one to blame   the rain

AS MARY MAGDALENE

Yes, the harlotry was mine, not cash-exchanging but handing
over again and again the holiness I believed myself housed in,
hemmed in, trading with this hack and that hapless one,
for a ha'pennyworth's of fear with what I called a dose
of happiness, but I was hardy, hearty, not long
haunted by the heaving and heart-sickness, the heedless,
headlong haunch-and-raunch, all thigh and hip and hind, this body
of mine—*come on Hotspur, show me your horsemanship, release your hounds
and ride*—I was holy, holey, wholly this heaviness, flattened
against the horsehair mattress. The kingdom and the glory.
What I thought I wanted was the temple destroyed.

ON CHARTRES STREET

between St. Louis Cathedral and the Slave Exchange
> find the Right Reverend Reverie and his SacraBand
>> drum strapped to his back
drop a dollar in the bucket
> his cymbals shimmer shut
> *a fool and her money*
sink of sin sheepfold   he slurs   *get thee to Ursuline*
>> Our Lady of Prompt Succor
> with her gold door   and her chapel made of bones

in St. Lucy's apothecary the virgin-martyr newly-sighted behind wire-rims
>> her face's silverbridge
> sings *vraiment, vraiment*
in her hands a boning knife an encyclopedia of cuts
>> the proverb that sustains you the precipitate of
>>> fear is
she separates florets for the fry pan   knowledge
> ask to be unsheltered
> *open the shutters*   *entre nous*
>> she says

9

My mother named me *small light*,
        called me Lucifer, light-bringer,
                too proud to follow.
She was a beauty, hair loaded
        high on her head, luxurious bow
                of lips.
Her artist painted my pale eyes on a platter,
        hers, cinder-dark, in my "restored" face.

She believed in the burlesque,
                the striptease, the slow burn.
Lucy, diminutive of light,
        the light-ess, the lightest,
                the light's test:
I am the lithe match,
        I will not strike.

in the shotgun bookstore   finger the water-warped edges
       to be a freethinker   possessed of Ulysses' desire to wander
Penelope's to wait   take only what is thrown
              coins   pearls   cups   cabbages
    the novels   sad Radclyffe   cannot prepare you
              for this shuddering

    in the narrow channel of Ms. Mae's   a body's width between stool and wall
    slosh quarters into the jukebox   *Brown-eyedGirl BandofGold*
Rosalind and her honeyman enter   he sings
           and I will hang around as long as you will let me
       your favorite song
     the pirogue of her hipbones

walk home alone at dawn
         by the stars on the manhole cover
as last night is washed with a hiss into the gutter
    in the window of the charcuterie   ducklings recto   pig snout verso
       at the auction house Louis XV   not Madame Right Now

AS MADAME MAINTENANT

I am that which does not persevere, the feminine rhyme, all those unstressed
syllables lining up behind, obscuring, usurping—

outside *la maison, le château,* I am maligned, I know

every monk, every organ grinder and mange-eaten monkey, every
sausage-maker mincing gizzards mumbles

Madame, Mistress, whoremonger, whore. Some midsummer's kiss

misconstrued, I'm misheard, I misstep, mis-
take what is not mine or am misled, and I am missing, a miss

taken away, no use wishing otherwise: we all slip

the manacles of time, eventually; no one really
wants to be the Sibyl—milky-eyed, misshapen, murmuring

I want to die. I'll wear the moss gown, be your

memento mori: femur, finger bone, skull. Muffler,
silk muzzle, amputated tongue. *La Mort, la merde. Mais oui,*

I am as ready as I'll ever be.

AS THOMAS, DOUBTING

I was not his twin. I tried to listen: be tenantless,
he said, Mary was male like us and could enter
the kingdom. Mary: tanned and touched
too thoroughly. He kissed her on the mouth.
To me, he said, you think too much. See what is
in front of you. But when I looked there
was nothing. Not nothing: thorn and thicket. Thomas,
he said, his thumb against my temple, you know
the difference between tender and tenderness.
It is not enough to be in thrall. Be a passerby.

XY:

Consider the Mound-lily Yucca (*y. gloriosa*)—not to be confused with the Spanish Bayonet (*y. aloifolia*), which will puncture your jeans and your thigh underneath: why are you worried about how attractive you are? The point is to conserve water. The yucca is a vascular plant: xylem and phloem, not heart fluttering. One can adapt to lack. The root can be pounded to soapy lather. Spread more zinc-oxide on your nose, dear: X marks the spot with a dot, dot, dot.

XX:

Why do you tell me what I already know? Oh ye of little faith, must you see to believe the Y-coordinate, the yield in widgets? I accept your preference for the vertical but not the zero-sum. I'm not quarrelling: *yes* is not the same as *not no*. The nuns caution: Xavier's severed arm hangs in a Vatican chapel: sunk costs cannot be recovered. Q: St. Francis or Frances? A: I could be your boy: let me turn for you: kiss my nape. O can be origin or null. Why? Why not?

XZ:

Consider the zipper, my now-zero, my once-zillion. Let's call you X and me Y. If Y wagers her vanity against X's unwillingness to touch her…No. Let's revise: if Y plots her ultimatum against X's vacillation, on what plane will they part? Usury: an unconscionable interest or the interlocking teeth without the sliding pull? Tell me of zone defense and I'll tell you of the great divisions of the earth's surface: Frigid, Temperate, and Torrid. I will be the zeroth in your series: the all for naught.

AS ST. THOMAS, CALLED DIDYMUS (THE TWIN)

Vultures are not buzzards—buzzards are hawks—and that wings-spread
stance is the heraldic pose

> and what does a name mean or change?

New world vultures have the weak, chicken-like feet of storks and ibises.
They vomit in self-defense: a free offering of the undigested

> for years, I thought St. Anastasia was a Romanov, and this
> boarded-up school named for her, well, explain again, the differ-
> ence between *to* and *to be*—as in *condemn* and *condemned*—

This venue of turkey vultures waits for the morning's first warm updraft

> and the difference between the *awful power of god* and *divine justice?*

Vultures riding thermals, rising in slow circles, are called a *kettle*: they move
like bubbles in a boiling pot

> my missing twin, I believe only in the discrepancy between what
> is and what is said.

the huckster's pompadour   her Medusa tattoo   let her read your cards
Fool   *Death*   *Queen of Cups*
your life's 'bout to change, gal   let her teach you   how to use your hands
her thumb   index finger   palm
against your clavicle   in your jugular notch   areola to armpit
the stink of skin   tally the tender bruises   keep the receipt   repeat

RING

the penny means wealth   no the penny means poverty the dime
means wealth   no the dime means call me ring me up dear   the
ring means married within a year but the thimble means married
never   that's not a thimble it's a cup   buy me a drink love   no the
next round's on you   the fleur-de-lis means love will bloom no it
will travel but return soon no it will scorn you   that's the button
scorn sweethearts all forlorn you're an old maid or a bachelor
born   anchors aweigh my dear the anchor's hope if you pull it
you'll be adrift   so there

AS EVE

His eagerly, my eagerness. He was older and, as they say, endowed
by the creator: the earl of earliness, of earthlier pleasures.

He had rough elbows, an earring in his left ear. What I wanted
was experience.

Not love. An exquisite exposure:
the image floating up from the emulsion.

Eros or error or
his sad story: estranged, expelled from his father's esteemed estate, etcetera.

He invited me to eat, showed me his
artifacts, the rib of an earthenware vase.

I was surprised, as I had been when I first touched a snake,
to find it dry.

That last evening of my not-knowing, I asked, who
is exacting, what is eternal, what everlasting?

He echoed the radio: love and evermore. He called me
earnest. Earn for short.

He entreated. He entered. And I was
the epithet, the epitaph, the epilogue

and then the exit. We existed (or at least I thought we did).
What a difference a day and an s, well placed, make.

EPITHALAMIUM: AFTER LORINE NIEDECKER

The women leave the limo
clasping lilies, led
by the groomsmen, one grasps
the maid of honor's gilded
arm like a glass stem. Aren't

lilies funeral flowers? Good
lord, look at the rock
on her finger. He's loaded,
right? Is there a rule about brides
over thirty-five and white? She's

not a shoe, this isn't Labor
Day, what should she wear? green?
lily pad or frog,
glistening? Not gossamer,
of course, but what? tulle,

taffeta, sateen? the color
of fertility, a totem
like the cornstalk
fence around the reception
hall? That gown isn't

white, it's *cornsilk* or *candlelight*.
How much older is he
than her? Than *she*? Please,
he's not quite old enough to be
her father, may he rest in peace.

The groom and the bride's
mother mug for the camera, her fist
against his jaw: "hurt my baby,"
she says, "and
I'mnotkiddingyou you're dead."

She draws in the windshield's dust a cow
near a carriage, a bird, inverted w, in flight,
which he takes to mean she's adjusted: addition

and subtraction: sometimes a body drops what it might
hold, the way he, bent over the addition's roof,
dropped nails when he coughed his smoker's cough and she

startled as if the church bell had tolled, had told,
had told, how many times had he been told that
chicken wire and peg board were not proper offerings,

but as acid believes in metal, he believes that the cord
to God is built with the detritus of this life, drain mesh,
copper tubing, twist ties: you tithe what you must: he sees

when she cries over the kitchen sink, her ear beautiful
though scarred where the earring ripped free
long ago: division and multiplication:

molasses slips from the edge of the spoon,
the cracked egg sticks to its paper cradle.

He's on the doorstep, wanting a drink and
a ride—as always, she's too happy to oblige:
she invites him in, but he won't cross that

threshold again: water—immersion—
is what he craves, but the paper said
the pool was closed, contaminated by what

she can't remember: she suggests a motel
or any body of water not ringed by chain link:
immersion and home, he says, his head's

been shaved, he doesn't remember the way: she
offers the clawfoot tub bolted to the kitchen floor
and kettle after kettle of water warmed and, on

the Formica table, gin, cigarettes, burnt
edges of newsprint—but the woman in black
clutching the tricornered flag, the woman

the paper called a window, a winnowing wind, his
widow is waiting, he says. The newspaper said
DOA and something about a rigged doorway.

"Finally, if a painting is good, it will be mostly memory."
—Andrew Wyeth

She is about to dissolve, a goddess
in her cape coat, a shower
of gold. *Overflow* began with her
standing, unclothed, of course, in front
of the linen cupboard. Restless he lay
her down in the slender bed, white-washed
the sheets and sill, left her arm reaching.
Of his wife in *Distant Thunder* he said, "Too much
face—I painted in the hat." In the storm-light
the dog glaring, his wife sleeping, and each
gold strand of grass blowing.

PHYSIOGNOMY

Your high forehead your dark arched brows your gold-flecked eyes so lustrous brown I say they are a sign of your quick mind and because I hold your gaze my good taste (not for me the obvious blue) that pointed chin that firm jaw line must mean wit mean grace and let's be honest some real stubbornness yes I don't always get my way let's call that strength of character moral fortitude but what do we do about your eyes in someone else's face let's not call it infidelity let's call it a sign of my admiration for your (her) mind and my good taste and remember dear the neat seam of your mouth (and mine) means a tendency toward measured speech or secrecy so let us not admit this impediment your lustrous eyes in someone else's face no my eyes on someone else's (beautiful) face.

I know you're wrecked   call me "mermaid" when you mean
you cannot abide my oceany stench   going on about my eyes
my eyes and the pearls   on the wife's neck
                No I don't know
what wainscoting is   for fuck's sake I'm shucking oysters
                          from their shells
Put down the tea and   the creased photo of your wife
on your wedding day   Yes she's pretty if peaked
I don't know how much more welcoming a girl could be
                   I've winked   I've wiped
the bar in front of you clean
                Why are you weeping over a peach
If the skin wrinkles under your finger   the flesh is ripe
juicy and sweet   goodness you're squeamish   about what's wet
If you say so   I can see how the napkin looks like a winding sheet
No you're not whining but   hurry up now please it's time

WHAT HAVE YOU GONE AND DONE

I leaned against the smelted grate, she kneeled
      on the concrete:
         we unsoldered the iron gate
             of mate and merge, her mouth
          on the verge of my median, that short
                         weave. She drove,
    I rode
        the trolley home.

     Not trolley, streetcar.

        I can't say
           I didn't because I did.
               I won't say
       what will be will be
            after three cheap drinks
         under the green awnings of Que Sera—

     Not median, neutral ground.

What's done is done. This
          is my stop: neutral
    ground, avenue, eight blocks
     of cracked sidewalk,
    an iron gate, unlocked.

This is where I get off.

Under this sun, hung this day so low and close,
you raise your hand to shade your eyes,
which are not suns or jewels but what they are:
brown-gold irises, pupils contracting:
the sun? or are you underwhelmed or angered
by what I've said or done? Might it be my
leg jiggling under this picnic bench or the angle
at which I look like your mother or that phrase
I used that reminds you of my ex, plucking
the fruit from the low hanging branch? I raise
my hand to better see. In your own created shade,
you say, again, it's nothing, it's not you; it's me—and turn
away, lifting your hand from my knee, to give me
your ear, which your genes have carved so delicately.

Your skin's glossy, sun-tight; your swim trunks drift
    below your hipbone in the pink light of late afternoon. I pinch
    the plump leaf of the rubber plant; you scrape the motel's
stucco. Your eyes are on the frontage road. A vulture floats
over the orange grove. Herons and egrets trail a tractor, snap up
    the frogs leaping clear. The succulents sprout in stones.
    I shear the aloe of its spars, slice it to spread on your blistered
skin. But for me to touch you, we must go in.

AT THE EXHIBIT ON FEMININE IDENTITY

you stand between the Sally Manns and Lorna Simpson's *She*

your back to me your ass tight-packed in your old jeans

trim green jacket square-toed shoes all ornament all beautiful

I swear I would love you in a dress but ah the skin exposed

when I slip buttons of horn from tight buttonholes

and kiss your wrists listing in French cuffs from the angle of muscle

where thumb becomes palm becomes hand becomes yes

AS ALICE ON GERTRUDE'S LAP

Not on. Abreast. A breast is abetting and aiding. A broach, a breast, un-clasped abuts a button. Accoutrement, accessory, a necessary country. A dress addressed, a red awry. A wry grey adored.

Ardor our door. The address not unknown. A knock. The (too) many who adore you.

An accident, a vase accosted, a cost, a breaking and a mending. Amend-ments and administrations. Aspersions and aspic. A tone, a meant tone. Atonement: cold meats on a platter, the placating cheese (there is no excuse). Attraction a traction. Ask again and I'll stay.

ANCHOR

bent   not quite nose to knee   I am eight this
place nursing home   clutches me   I clutch the present
a carnation in my sweaty hand   cannot prevent   my wrist
against the wheel of her chair her knee   the nun chides   presses
me toward the hand like hide   the wrist like a turtle's neck
in a dirty sleeve   the gnarled hand that clutches me   I wish
I could have been a better child   not afraid of everything   we are
here to sing   some variation on the theme of waiting   we begin
silent night   I am not calm in these bright halls   *'round yon*
years from this   a man is wheeled by my mother's door   his mouth
stuck open as if yelling   my god   my father sighs
wishes for his own quick death   says come along now   she needs her rest

In the whorl of woodgrain, the hag, kerchiefed, sharp-chinned,
or the young woman upswept hair, long necked, not looking?

An Alzheimer's patient pets the daughter's arm: *Pretty, why
are those people parking in our yard? where is our father?*

And the multitude said, *behold, your mother is looking
for you*, and the answer came, *Who is my mother?*

On the aide's radio, Prince sings, *maybe you're
just like my mother. She's never*

What she learned from her mother:
Ladies do not *sweat*, they *perspire*.

In the courtyard, the daughter lifts a blade of grass to the chicken-wire cage;
the green shivers in the rabbit's teeth, shimmies and is gone.

Pallid majesty—opalescent beauty—I'm kneeling
on this tile floor, asking for her restoration: give her back
the language in which she names me. Is there a sentence
you regret revoking?

Dread queen, if she cannot be wheeled
from this ward, will you tell me if she perceives, but dimly, each
word as it is offered? What if I bring blankets
and morphine? What if I look away?

AS EURYDICE, APHASIC

Absence inhabits my mouth. [orchard, phantom]

calls, *your, rid, dust, see?* I do

not follow. Fevered [orphan, porous]

presses ice to my slack lips, uncurls

my fingers from my fist. *fell*

low fall oh. He does not want

to see me like this. [or fear us]

look at me, I want

to say. Look.

While she admits gravity has it charms, keeping sugar
in its bowl, she envies smoke its plumes, the insouciant curl,
the lasso's lift and the rope's whirl against the gloved hand

rather than the lariat's cinching 'round the neck; of course,
drills whir and water funnels down, but it's not the swirling

really, not room-slipping dizziness or the old shuffle of 33s
in the jukebox she wants but the fumes at the periphery
of the gas pump, the shimmer on a hot day, the possibility

of ascension, of translucence, of the light passing through
the murk of her, clock-bound, in a narrow room.

She played "Greensleeves," her fingernails clicking on the ivory keys. *Alas, my love, my gosling, my silly goose*. She took me to the pond to feed her swans, all guile and aggression, their tail feathers *lurid*, she said, *in the original sense, a ghastly pale yellow*.

❧

In her cedar chest, my inheritance: a rabbit fur glove, lurid in the original sense, ghastly pale yellow, her wedding dress, and a red leather bible, gilt-edged.

❧

She met me at the gate, early one morning, *to cast me off*. Yes, I was drunk and lurid, in the later sense, glaring, glowing. The gleam of sex. The stink and steam of it. A lass, my love. Sunlit mist above the brackish pond.

❧

The amber husk of a bee clings to the cemetery's one tree. In my arms, an ivory urn, gold-handled. Behind the columbaria, the bank of ash, a snakeskin sloughed, no, a condom snagged, in the grass. A body, Mother, cannot be uncast.

IN ANNA GASKELL'S UNTITLED #6 (WONDER)

I am jumping, no

      falling, fingers and feet

spread, small bosom

      sheathed in a yellow

dress, my blue apron

      twisting, the hem caught

against cotton stockings—

      Snow White or Rose

Red but without shoulders

      or head, only the dark

green of trees, the leaves

      spattering.

IN CATHERINE OPIE'S SELF-PORTRAIT / CUTTING

who has razored
the physics of the drip

       on the skin of her back, two women
       slit waists, pronged legs, triangular skirts

underscoring the illusion of an ordinary
life, a clutch of secrets

a mother might pass on

did I say mother

       the beading birds above, I meant
       house over which settles

multiple models of doubt, did I say drip

       the idea of home, I meant rot

I meant meager plot.

I sat on stone benches carved into the hillside, waiting
for the moment night
      began—
the rotation, the light pulling
      back like the tide—and though I lived
by the charts
      (sunrise at 6:38)
so much remained unseen—
                    as under waves,
      the currents' turning—

and then one small bat pulled
      from the mouth of the cave
by night —
      like a child's rubber toy jerked
on a string—into the grey wash,
      the change unmarked in the firmament
            (no high-tide line)—

then two, then ten, then hundreds (motes
                   in an updraft),
each out to eat its thousand insects,
      and sooner than I'd hoped
the inability to discern
           body or wing
                    from sky.

DENIAL, TRIPTYCH

I.

The child asks. They say, *don't*. A sparrow
    pecks at the frozen ground. Her father's
letter, a spasm of words she can't

understand. Her doll swathed
    in Irish lace. The hem
of the old mother's skirt shivers.

Her young mother lifts the needle,
    plays again the ballad: *Hush, Child.* The parlor
is cleared for the coffin.

II.

In the old mother's bible, Bellini's risen Christ, ravished
    by dying, staggers against the pale sky; His dark lips,
the nipple revealed by the rent O of His gown are the same

iron oxide red as the beading on His brow; Mantegna's Christ lies
    bluing, a foreshortened cadaver: puncture wounds cleaned, the winding
sheet unwound to reveal the beauty of His body from sternum

to pubis. To the priest, the old mother says *accident* and *casket closed.*
    The child smooths the ripples from the rug and prays
for the souls in purgatory as she's been told.

III.

At the edge of the ice-thick pond, a web
    of white scratched into black
as in Doré's etching of souls frozen skull-deep

in hell. The caption, as her father read it, *Take good heed*
    thy soles tread not on the heads of thy brethren.
She hears the echo of ice cracking, not cracking.

To get home, she is told, she must cross
    the ice. She gives the answers
she knows: *No thank you*, and, *thank you, no.*

Mother

In the parlor, an open book, a wood-tipped pen, and alongside her
son, two jars of flowers and a priest too young to understand. *Let not*
the wind or the grass take the barefoot boy he once was
in the dark, in the barn, from under the back porch as his *father*
did, beating him in the name of, *in the name of* all that was *holy*
that boy could hide (woman after woman)—where did he spend
the war? on his grandmother's farm, now boarded up, now gone to *dust?*

Daughter

Aluminum can blasted from the fence. Alongside her *father*, the fine
print. Even he would permit the wind is not evil, the untended field
becomes meadow. A tipped bucket on the back porch, casings, shells. He left
his name, the smell of gunpowder, ragweed and hay, boxes of bees, an orchard
of switches, denuded. *He hath joined* the sect of the grass. The lesson
of the *son* of man: desertion.

Wife

cross of tin   him   two cups   of whiskey   bucket of ash
bucket of seed   wind-shed   death takes   a man to pasture
he maketh me to lie down   in the name of   new headstone   old plot
no headstone   metal plate   what burns   not the box   the body
not the box   crops fail *holy* from disease sterility neglect   *ghost*

He was going to chalk, sir.
His favored rebukes: so sue
for mercy, go soak in petrol.
He said he would not guard
the sacristy, or tie orchids
to the lady's feet, that dame,
Time, so perky and sure of
herself. He said I was common
as dolor, as the word *love* tattooed.
Father, if his brain was rimed
and lacey with the disease, he
still loved his bees, a cocktail
at five, the smell of paint, and
that chintz settee. Christ, his
kids? I don't know— I'd like
to cast my vote, sir, for the idea
of family but I'm jet-lagged
and still too many time zones away.

DIMINUTIVES WITH SNAPSHOTS

Wiflet

His not-yet father hunches over his not-yet mother. His hands almost meet around her brocaded waist. She holds his dangling tie in two fists. He is shiny with sweat and laughing. Maybe they have been dancing. Their fingers are bare.

> Later, when he is almost a man and before some court, an official will say, "she was his mistress."

> "No, sir," he'll reply, "There is a better word, an older word, that word is *wife*, common law. But for years at a time, she was my mother and only mine."

Puppykin

A gold dog by the door of a blue convertible, the cocker spaniel his mother
called Honey, who, she said, loved to ride at her feet.

>After the quarantine, when Honey was stranded
>for twelve weeks at some port between here
>and there, she whined at every crate, cage, and gate.

Firstling

A rutted dirt road, breast-high grass (wheat or oats) on either side. At the curve, a red speck, a fox worrying a burrow.

> He is told he traveled with his father once, when he was
> six, maybe seven. He has no memory of it but somewhere he
> learned of happiness: you can sustain it if you don't stay overlong.

Motherlet

On a sea wall, in a white shirt-dress, gold sandals,
a straw handbag beside her, his mother, not smiling.

> This he remembers: he swam until the waves ate the pebbled shore,
> until they licked the wall. Nothing more.

Motherling

The pocket of her apron, an embroidered owl
with orange eyes, her pale fingernail,

> her singing a language he did not speak. From her translation, he'd
> made a story: *A mouse disappeared in a city. His brother-friend seeking him*
> *found the one who gave him shelter. She'd had a squirming brood by then. She*
> *swept the mat that he might sleep outside her door. A cat carried him away.*
>
> He loved the refrain, *carried, carried, carried him away*, so he is
> startled, later, by what it means.

Lastling

Blurred terrazzo floor and, perhaps, the tip of one black shoe.

> She was young when she became his mother and young when she
> ceased to be. Once, on the sidewalk home from school, he did not
> see her in a mud-colored wig until she called him by his name.

a pendant, a cord in clear light. Lace shadow. Listen, rays of light, listen. Raze, raise my son and my non-son, my outrage. Make them praise me.

My wife's ancient orange cat hunches over the vent, a burning bush. Hairs, a billion flames, tour the filthy floor. Out of doors, a tomcat lows his verse and refrain.

At the long feedtrough, éclairs and white fish, the other ill gent, vain still, dried egg on his vest, pockets out like tents. He's keyless. No souvenirs of ceilings

he once owned. Descend, Lord, descend. Break this, this, the aide dressing me, her hands shoving my shirt into my pants. Lord, I'm stranded in this port, sore

of sleeping. Sore. The éclairs rest. Tents of pastry, mush I'd be rid of, much I'd be rid of, her face in that frosted casket.

ONE MORE THING (A POEM IN WHICH I PRAY TO WHOM I KNOW NOT)

For the attendant to tend the reviled sheets.

To the memory of clean.

For the curb to arrest the dawn.

To keep it from clamoring in the bedroom with its clear and boring story.

For her key to find your door.

To her not to quit firmly and depart for good this time.

For this audience, the animals I care for so you can rest, to be saved: No one goes to the market, or we all go, one by one, for slaughter.

I ENTER WITH BAIL MONEY, BUT YOU CAN'T BE SPRUNG

A triangle of trotters clank against the glass, jarred in vinegar, pinker
than the clerk's fake fingernails. Behind the bristling counter, the ample ass
of night, a million celluloid lips, rouged and waiting, to give suck, a million
rough teats.

The back office volleys with me, calls this casket a coupe, a coup, a bargain
to raise the dead from their tombs. I rest in the illusion, attractive
in that instant, like the face of a pig, joyful, against a fence.

On the way to the mound, the burial ground, I regard my prayers
as droll decorations, embroidered wall hangings: bless this mess.

IF YOU SEE SOMETHING, SAY SOMETHING

Something raises the raccoons, their mute snouts, above the garbage pail, looking like police or little trees on a grey horizon. They head for the trees, their menacing heads swinging.

The courier honks his long horn. He carries something along the wall. Some thing arrives in the long drought. Ashes. Volatile air. The route of my brother, I envy; he's a medic with a trophy heart, an atrophied heart he keeps in a bottle. Meat, he says, we are all meat.

Something comes to the window. I open the door. I am, as you have always found me, wanting.

"Wedding Pulls" incorporates a bit of a Victorian saying associated with the custom of pulling charms from the wedding cake: "The thimble for an old maid or bachelor born; The button for sweethearts all forlorn."

"As Mary Magdalene," "As St. Lucy," "As Thomas, Doubting," "As Madame Maintenant," "As Eve," "As the Wench," and "As Alice on Gertrude's Lap" draw language from a wiktionary of all the words used in Shakespeare's plays and poems: http://en.wiktionary.org/wiki/Wiktionary:Frequency_lists/ Complete_Shakespeare_wordlist

"Son, I Lie," "One More Thing," "I Enter With Bail Money, But You Can't Be Sprung," and "If You See Something, Say Something" began as homophonic translations of poems in Pierre Reverdy's *Flaques de Verre*.

The quotations in "Too Much Face" were taken from Andrew Wyeth: Remembrance, Seattle Art Museum, June 25-October 18, 2009.

Other bits, borrowings, echoes, and inspirations: * Shakespeare's Sonnet 116 and Sonnet 130 * Gertrude Stein's *Tender Buttons* * T.S. Eliot's "Wasteland" & "The Love Song of J. Alfred Prufrock" * Psalm 23:2 * Mark 3:32 * Marvin Meyer's translation of the Gospel of St. Thomas * John Keat's "To Autumn" * Prince's "When Doves Cry" * "Silent Night"

ACKNOWLEDGEMENTS

My enduring thanks to the editors of the following journals and anthologies who first published these poems:

1913: a journal of forms: "Wedding Pulls" and "In Catherine Opie's Self Portrait / Cutting"
Beltway Poetry Quarterly: "In the Xeriscape" and "As Alice on Gertrude's Lap"
Best New Poets, 2011 (Judge: D.A. Powell): "On Decatur Street," "On Chartres Street," "On Esplanade Avenue," "On Magazine Street," "On St. Charles Avenue," originally published as "Unmapped."
Calyx: "As Thomas, Didymus the Twin" and "As the Prodigal Sister"
Gargoyle: "As Mary Magdalene"
ILK: "As the Wench"
Lavender Review: "Genealogy"
New Orleans Review: in print "As Eve," "As St. Thomas, Doubting" & online "As St. Lucy," "As Madame Maintenant"
The Northern Virginia Review: "Epithalamium: After Lorine Niedecker"
Queer South Anthology: "What Have You Gone and Done" and "As the Prodigal Daughter"

I am grateful to and for my dear mentors and friends who helped shape the poems and the manuscript: Sally Keith, Eric Pankey, Jennifer Atkinson, Susan Tichy, Zofia Burr; the Grrls—Martha Kreiner, Katherine Williams, Katherine Gekker, Mariah Burton Nelson, Michelle Mandolia, Lawrence Biemiller; and my GMU & Heritage Workshop peers. My gratitude, too, to Northern Virginia Community College for the educational leave and George Mason University for the Completion Fellowship; to Shannon Johnson Uschold for her friendship and the space in NOLA to write; to Joan Houlihan, Martha Rhodes, and my Colrain cohort for their bracing advice; to SLS and Eileen Myles for Lithuania; to Meg Reid, Betsy Teter, and Eric Kocher for the prize, the press, and their kindness; to my family for their love and support; for all and above all, Karen Murph.

Finally, I am utterly indebted to C.D. Wright for her selection of this manuscript for the New Southern Voices Poetry Prize and for all that her poems and prose have taught me.

The New Southern Voices Book Prize was established in 2013 and is a biennual prize awarded to an emerging Southern poet who has published at most one previous collection of poetry. It is awarded for a book-length collection of poems written originally in English.

 **HUB CITY**
PRESS

HUB CITY PRESS is a non-profit independent press in Spartanburg, SC that publishes well-crafted, high-quality works by new and established authors, with an emphasis on the Southern experience. We are committed to high-caliber novels, short stories, poetry, plays, memoir, and works emphasizing regional culture and history. We are particularly interested in books with a strong sense of place.

Hub City Press is an imprint of the non-profit Hub City Writers Project, founded in 1995 to foster a sense of community through the literary arts. Our metaphor of organization purposely looks backward to the nineteenth century when Spartanburg was known as the "hub city," a place where railroads converged and departed.

HUB CITY PRESS poetry

Punch • Ray McManus

Pantry • Lilah Hegnauer

Waking • Ron Rash

Eureka Mill • Ron Rash

Checking Out • Tim Peeler

Twenty • Kwame Dawes, editor

Home Is Where • Kwame Dawes, editor

Still Home • Rachel Harkai, editor

Voodoo For the Other Woman • Angela Kelly